MECCA, BAGHDAD, CORDOBA
AND MORE
THE MAJOR CITIES OF ISLAMIC RULE

HISTORY BOOK FOR KIDS
Past and Present Societies

CONTENTS

In this book, we're going to talk about the major cities of Islamic rule.

So, let's get right to it!

The empire of the Islam religion grew to become one of the largest kingdoms of the ancient world. As the empire expanded, towns grew into very populated cities that were hubs of importing and exporting. Many of these cities had special religious significance.

The city of Mecca and the city of Medina were two of the cities that had importance because of the religious history of Islam. Some cities were primarily important due to the fact that the rulers and government officials, known as the Caliphate, were located there. People who worship according to the Islam religion are described as Muslims.

Islamic family at a mosque in Mecca.

Mecca, Saudi Arabia.

1

MECCA

Mecca, located in modern-day Saudi Arabia, is the city with the most significance to Muslims. It is located 45 miles to the east of the city of Jedda, which is a port on the Red Sea encircled by the Sirat Mountain range.

The city of Mecca is known to Muslims as Umm al-Qura, which means the "Mother of Cities." This is the birthplace of the prophet Muhammad so for Muslims the city is holy ground. Muhammad was born in Mecca in the year 570 CE.

No matter where Muslims are living or working all over the world, they face Mecca when they pray during their five sessions of prayer each day. Mecca was the most important location in ancient times and it still is today.

Most able-bodied Muslims who have the sufficient income to do so must make

Muslim pilgrims perform saei (brisk walking) from Safa mount to Marwah mount.

Muslim pilgrims from all over the world gathered to perform Umrah or Hajj at the Haram Mosque in Mecca.

a religious journey to Mecca once during their lifetimes. This journey to Mecca to visit the Sacred Mosque is called the hajj and takes place during the twelfth lunar month of Dhu-al-Hijah.

The Sacred Mosque encircles the Ka'aba, which is a cube-like structure that Muslims believe was built by Abraham and his son. Abraham is an important figure in the Islam religion as well as in Christianity and Judaism.

Muhammad was born into a wealthy family and he married a wealthy woman who had many caravans. Muhammad managed her caravans until he had a spiritual experience at the age of 40.

He went up to Mount Hira and began to meditate while he was in a cave. It was there that he had a series of visions, which Muslims believe were given to him by Gabriel, the archangel.

Eventually, Muhammad would be given many mystical revelations.

The Qur'an, the holy book of the Islamic religion, contains the messages that Muslims

Kaaba in Masjid Al Haram in Mecca, Saudi Arabia.

believe Gabriel gave to Muhammad. However, when Muhammad began teaching these messages to the citizens

of Mecca, they not only rejected him, but they treated him with hostility.

Mecca's holy mosque in Saudi Arabia.

2

MEDINA

Located in modern-day Saudi Arabia, the city of Medina is the second most holy city to Muslims after Mecca. In 622 CE, Muhammad fled to the city of Medina, called Yathrib at that time, after he was persecuted and driven out of Mecca.

During the remainder of Muhammad's life, the city of Medina was the Islamic Empire's capital city. The first Caliphs reigned from Medina.

Muhammad preached in Medina for eight years and his followers began to grow in numbers very quickly. He then returned to his birthplace with an army. He wanted to cleanse the sacred Ka'aba of idols that were pagan.

Over the centuries, the Ka'aba had become defiled with pagan idols and Muhammad wanted to re-dedicate it to Allah, the one

The tomb of the Islamic prophet Muhammad and early Muslim leaders, Abu Bakar and Umar.

God of the Islamic religion.

The Ka'aba holds a mysterious black stone. There are many stories about the stone. It may be a meteorite.

One story is that the stone was from heaven and that it was white originally. It became black as it absorbed the sins of mankind. Muslims don't worship this stone. They pay homage to it because Muhammad did so.

Kaaba in Masjid Al Haram in Mecca, Saudi Arabia.

In 632 CE, Muhammad spoke to over 30,000 followers on the plains of Mount Arafat. After he taught the assemblage, he stated that his earthly mission was now complete.

He died in the city of Medina two months later. Within a century, the religion of Islam had spread from the European country of Spain to the country of India.

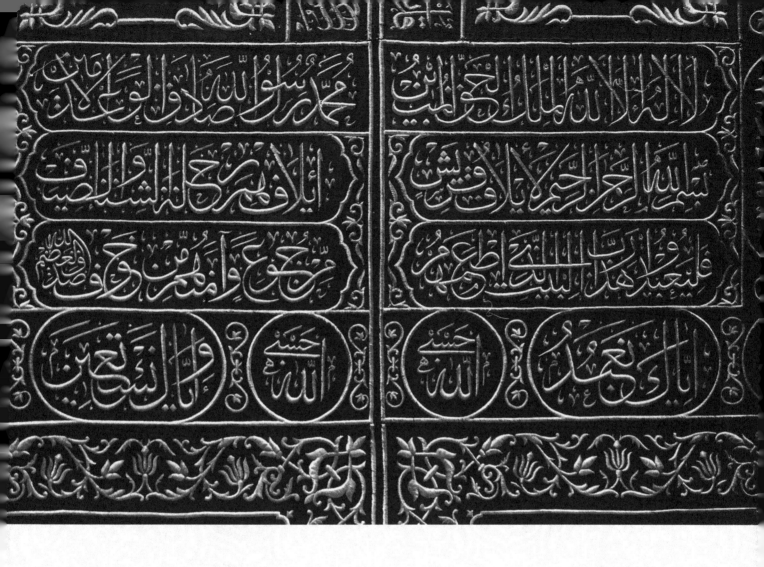

Today, many Muslim pilgrims come to Medina to pay homage at Muhammad's tomb there.

 Arabic script on the black cover of the "black stone".

28

Both Mecca and Medina are designated only for people of the Islamic religion. If non-Muslims are found within the limits of these cities, they are immediately deported. The city of Medina is called the *"City of the Prophet."*

Muslims walking in front of the mosque of the Prophet Muhammad in Medina, Saudi Arabia. Prophet's tomb is under the green dome.

The Dome of the Rock (Qubbet el-Sakhra) is one of the greatest Islamic monuments, it was built by Abd el-Malik, Jerusalem, Israel.

3

JERUSALEM

Jerusalem in modern-day Israel is the third most holy city to Muslims. Muslims used to align themselves for prayer in the direction of the city of Jerusalem until Muhammad was instructed to change that site to the city of Mecca.

The direction of prayer is called the *"qibla."* According to the Islam religion, Muhammad was transported to

Jerusalem after his death and ascended from that location into heaven.

The most important site to Muslims in the city is the Dome of the Rock, which is called Qubbat as-Sakhrah. Just like the Ka'aba, it is built over a stone that is considered to be sacred.

The stone there is sacred to Jews and Christians as well since this is thought to

Interior of Dome on the Rock on Temple Mount.

Mousque of Al-aqsa (Dome of the Rock) in Old Town - Jerusalem, Israel.

be the location where Abraham was ready to sacrifice his son as God had requested. The Dome of the Rock was constructed beginning in 685 CE.

4

DAMASCUS

The city of Damascus in modern-day Syria fell to the Islamic Empire in the year 634 CE. Formerly, the city had been part of the Eastern Roman Empire, which was called the Byzantine Empire. Under the Umayyad Caliphate, which ruled from 661 to 750 CE, the city of Damascus was made the capital city of the empire and it remained its political and trade hub for almost a century.

5

BAGHDAD

The Abbasids took over the empire in the year 750 CE. They decided to establish a new capital. They chose a location at the heart of Mesopotamia along the Tigris River, which became the city of Baghdad in modern-day Iraq.

Beginning in 762 CE, Baghdad was founded as the new center of governmental power. For the next five centuries, it was the most influential city in the Middle East. The city of Baghdad was one of the first planned cities worldwide.

Because Baghdad was a planned city, architects constructed the center of the city as a large circle and it was called the "Round City" as a result. Over half a million people were citizens of Baghdad by the 9th century. It had become one of the world's largest cities.

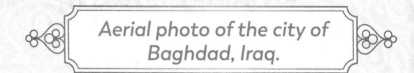

Aerial photo of the city of Baghdad, Iraq.

6

CAIRO

The Mongols overthrew the city of Baghdad in the year 1258 CE. They destroyed most of the city. The Abbasid Caliphate fled and established themselves in the city of Cairo in Egypt.

They remained the religious leaders of the Islamic world, but the governmental and political power was seized by the Mamluks.

The Mamluks had been the former slaves of the Abbasid Caliphate and they had risen up as an army of warriors.

Cairo became the hub of the Muslim population for several centuries after this event.

Mosque Madrassa of Sultan Hassan in Cairo, Egypt.

Panoramic view of the Blue Mosque with minarets.

7

CONSTANTINOPLE

The Ottomans overthrew the city of Constantinople in the year 1453. Then, in 1517, the Ottomans seized the city of Cairo and took over the Caliphate. At that time, Constantinople was one of the world's largest cities. It was a major trading hub. Today, the city is called Istanbul and it is located in modern-day Turkey.

8

CORDOBA

The city of Cordoba on the Iberian Peninsula was the hub of the Islamic Empire in the country of Spain as well as the country of Portugal.

At first, it was under the rule of the Umayyad Caliphate. However, it separated from the Umayyads when the Abbasid Caliphate came to power.

At one time, Cordoba was the capital

city of the Islamic government in the country of Spain. Al-Andalus was the name for the Muslim section of Spain during Medieval times.

During the Muslim reign of Cordoba, it became a very sophisticated city. It was more advanced than most of the other European cities. Its streets were very wide and they were also paved. The citizens had clean, running water.

Mihrab of the Mosque in Cordoba, Spain.

Roman Bridge and Guadalquivir River showcasing the Great Mosque - Cordoba, Spain.

They also had public hospitals and other modern amenities that other cities in Europe didn't have throughout the Middle Ages. In 1236 CE, during the Reconquista, the city of Cordoba returned to Christianity.

SUMMARY

The Islamic Empire established many great cities and became one of the largest empires of the world in ancient times. Mecca is considered to be the most holy city in all of Islam. It is the birthplace of Muhammad.

Originally, the citizens of Mecca were hostile to his teachings, so he fled to Medina, which is considered the second most holy city to Muslims. Eventually,

Muhammad returned to Mecca and established it as the direction of prayer for Muslims worldwide.

Awesome! Now that you've read about the major cities of Islamic rule, you may want to read about the rulers of Islam in the Baby Professor book *Umayyad, Abbasid and Ottoman Caliphates - Islamic Empire History Book 3rd Grade | Children's History.*

Visit

PROFESSOR BEAVER
Building Smarter and Brighter Minds

www.ProfessorBeaver.ca

to download Free Professor Beaver eBooks
and view our catalog of new and exciting
Children's Books

CPSIA information can be obtained
at www.ICGtesting.com
Printed in the USA
LVHW051252080323
741125LV00009B/746

9 780228 228684